LITTLE LILLY LITTLEFIELD'S
LITTLE BOOK OF POEMS

Donald Edward Webber

LITTLE LILLY LITTLEFIELD'S
LITTLE BOOK OF POEMS

Donald Edward Webber

Donald Edward Webber

About the Author

The author of *Little Lilly Littlefield's Book of Poems* attended St. Olaf College, Luther Theological Seminary, and The New England Synod School of Lay Ministry. He has taught, coached, and served as a private college Admissions Director and Development Officer.

He also functioned as Chairman, President, CEO and COO of mutual fund sales and marketing companies in Boston, Chicago, and New York City.

The author spent 10 years of his life managing a genetic predisposition to chronic, major depressive disorder in the mid 90s and into the beginning of the 21st Century. Poems attributable to depression are found under the heading, The Dark Days. The author is an advocate of all mental health initiatives.

Retired, he now is a full-time Instructional Aide at his local high school working with traditional and non-traditional students.

He lives in Exeter, New Hampshire.

Artwork is the creation of:
Morgan Clinard and Linsey Kesslen

BLANKETS OF SNOW

Blankets of snow cover the fields today,
    The orchard, the pond, the rutted roadway.
Limbs hang heavy some touching the ground,
    Many have broken with cracking sounds.

Swirling flakes bring chilling designs,
    Now barn and coup are hard to find.
Trees are coated to the windward side,
    A few lonely leaves seem to jump and slide.

In the distance, a wall of white,
    Before it saplings appear so slight.
Hemlocks sway, together in song,
    Pines stand tall, anchored strong.

Roofs feel heavy, coated in waves,
    Drifts render doors tight to stay.
Windows are painted in fanciful art,
    Houses are dressed a color apart.

Blankets of snow cover the land today,
    Who ventures forth, one could not say.
Time to reflect, work past the storm,
    Time to collect, think a new dawn

Published in The Old Farmer's Almanac 2020

Donald Edward Webber

BACKYARDS IN SPRING

Apples trees in bloom,
    Sun on white petals, tinted pink.
        Breathe deep the sweet, sweet smell of spring.

Soon the peach, yes the pear,
    Blossoms light purple, pink and white as well.
        Aromas of honey, a narcotic trapping.

The arbor is stretching forth,
    Came the buds, covering the trellis.
        No more wind from the north.

The backyard, again a pond.
    Splashing down, arriving mallards and hens,
        In spring they sing their song.

Lilacs growing tall to the sill,
    Favorites, violet and light magenta.
        Scent heady, spicy, intense.

Yellow crocus gone, no lavender here.
    They came early, through the frost.
        Saffron, mostly in autumn.

Colors of the rainbow with a touch of cream,

Donald Edward Webber
Tulip season, even if short.
April usually, midst the showers.

Backyards in spring,
Soil so dark, smells cold and moist.
The gritty feel of new life.

CAN'T SEE THROUGH IT

Can't see through it, it's coming straight on,
Glistening on the water, the sun past dawn.
Sparkling, glimmering, dancing off waves,
Forcing a squint, first stumble of the day.

Leaving the horizon climbing the sky,
What first was blinding, now softer on the eye.
Settling above, seemingly on high,
Soon to clear mid-day, reckoning night.

Come late day, shadows are fixed,
Complete success, maybe mixed?
Direction was clearer, given light,
Look to drift easy, easy into night.

Darkness offers wonders, only if seen,
Hiding from light, all seems pristine.
The moon offers glimpses, need to beware,
Venture forth carefully, omens to bear.

Wonder if everything so startling and clear,
At first seems blinding, till through it one steers?
Wonder if waiting for light to shift,
Is nature's lesson, patience is a gift.

Donald Edward Webber

COLOR OF NIGHT

Walking a distance when I could not see,
Soon to discover a path ahead of me.
At first it was hiding providing no mark,
Until it gave way to a color so dark.

Moon was a sliver, low out of view,
Hidden by tree tops, hills I knew.
Time came to sit, prevent a fall,
Rest on my blanket, ease the pall.

Then gazing in the sky on such a clear night,
Searching for life, the movement of light.
Too many too count, too many too bright,
Remaining but captives to the color of night.

Closing my eyes looking at life,
In prayer and meditation to make it right,
Images and demons manifest a fright,
Immune to my escape from the color of night.

Waking too early long before dawn,
Listening to silence, my mind, the calm.
Without definition thoughts random as stars,
They quickly succumbed to the color afar.

Donald Edward Webber

FALL AGAIN

Fall again,
Colors are at their peak.
Breezes off the water are cooler,
Evenings are closer each week.

Mums are out in abundance,
Pumpkins spill off carts.
Doors are draped with cornstalks,
Leaves swirl around the parks.

Trees become nature's artwork,
Squirrels seem busier than before.
Couples bundle for long walks,
Skies are hazy no more.

Ponds look to be smoking,
Warnings midst the chill?
Cold out of the north again,
A seasonal chapter fulfilled.

Come fall again,
A favorite time of year.
Some have lived it many times,
Some never see their way clear.

Donald Edward Webber

FIRST OF SNOW

First of snow arrived today,
Some might think it early.
October leaves, dressed fresh white,
Grass, coated completely.

Squirrels tracks, easy to find,
Wild turkeys peck the ground.
Labs burrow noses where they can,
Sparrows circle round and round.

Hooves dig deep, grass is there,
Ruminants smell it, snorting harshly.
Bales of hale still in the barn,
Soon to be delivered, late but timely.

Little ones play with delight,
Elders brush and shovel.
The kids in us kick a path,
While others seem to struggle.

Air is crisp, paths are hid,
A time unlike another.
Soon the sun will take command,
Refreshing fall's deep color.

Donald Edward Webber

FROST CAME EARLY THIS FALL

Frost came early this fall,

Something about global warming.

Air smells intriguingly heavy,

Some windows need scraping.

Yesterday's grass so green, so soft,

Now crisp when walking upon.

Never certain how residual it is,

Cut and crushed, abused, and set on.

Little patches of ice a'foot, fun to crunch.

Crackle, pop, spongy underneath like a summer lawn.

Always looking for the perfect design,

Cracked ice, like a mirror gone wrong.

Snow up north, cold in the mountains,

Certainly not too surprising.

Just not ready here in the valley,

Sun still early in the east when rising.

Frost was light, no damage to flowers,

First concern with strays and the abandoned.

Donald Edward Webber

Feel the air when first stepping out,

Can't imagine the damned, sleeping in it.

Frost is early, surely a sign,

A harbinger, need to be ready.

Fall enters quickly, quietly changing a season,

Comes every year, rely on it, steady.

GONE AGAIN

Gone again,
Seems they came just yesterday.
Of course it's to be expected,
Yet the loss is felt anyway.

They came in spring softly,
Light greens and early limes,
Flowers hastened quickly,
Signaling it was their time.

Depths of color shown in summer,
With intensity proven to impress.
Soon we tasted fruits and seeds,
A fall season many treasure best.

In winter apple and pear stand bare,
Maples reach clean and high.
White oaks display empty arms,
Only pines still temper the sky.

Gone again,
With them we spent little time.
Seems they left without us,
The loss should serve to remind.

Donald Edward Webber

GONE THE POLAR WINDS

Gone are the long nights,
Chills to keep one awake.
Gone streaming polar winds,
Giving window and door to shake.

What came of the polar vortex?
Spilled her freeze and left.
Then split, she did, and turn away,
Leaving the land bereft.

Now feel the gentle breezes,
Warmth throughout they bring.
Carrying a familiar message,
Again the taste of spring.

Heavy and rich, season's fragrant soil,
Tilled deep while moist and firm.
Frost felt afoot, inching its rise,
Eager to give crocus its turn.

Come red breasted robins, too many to count,
Geese on wing, heading north.
Harbingers of change leading seasonal fronts,
Soft zephyrs soon, soon coming forth.

Selected verses in *The Old Farmer's Almanac 2021*

Donald Edward Webber

LEAVES OF LATE FALL

Weathered, faded, drying fast,

Driven in the sky with each breeze.

Crackling, dropping,

Blanketing the ground with ease.

Flame red on maple, yellow on birch.

Burnt orange on oak colored fast.

Lime on poplar, plum purple on ash,

Brown needles on pines fall last.

Wind driven showers weakens stems,

Hard rain pressures leaves.

Cold flurries shake, white flakes dress,

Snow covers soft in relief.

Chilled be the forest, broken limbs untold,

Blackened stumps remain of the fallen.

Listen for movement amidst a backdrop still,

Echoes only, falling leaves breathing.

Leaves of late fall captured aloft,

Donald Edward Webber

Swirling colors up then round.

Piles of and more, harboring the tired,

Journeying the season fast found.

STAND OF PINES

Stalwart soldiers, stationed strong,
Tall and weathered, seasons long.
Anchored deep, footings hold,
Breath of reach, branches bold.

Together Spartans, strength supports,
Command attention, presence reports.
Winds they buffer, sunlight shade,
Rain is softened, pinecones made.

Tapered tops, nature's hand,
King's Pines they beckon, on demand.
Reaching full, at their height,
Marshalling support, formation tight.

Depth of rank, dark and deep,
Forbade foolhardy, timid and weak.
Scars of honor, broken and cut,
Trails of fallen, pathways shut.

Blackened skeletons, prominence past,
Protrude from hillsides, positions last.
Void of life, headstone posture,
Amidst the thriving, intrigue they foster.

Donald Edward Webber

Beds of needles, a forests floor,
Through the wood, reach soft reach sure.
Tread with care, steps come quick,
Mark a path, trailways trick.

Stand of pines, signs of life,
Surviving time, midst calm and strife.

SUN AT DAWN

Peeking into a grayish sky,
Ablaze with blinding light,
She inches her way into command,
Warming the chill of the night.

Ocean breezes begin to take flight,
Gone quickly evening's darkened fright.
Waves arise, seagulls cry,
Little crabs scurry, they hide in a hurry.

Broken seashells once anchored tight,
Unseen they were in pale moonlight,
Waiting for waves to swoosh them away,
For seashells and driftwood, just another day.

Surf's astir, cool sea, warm temps collide,
Steady winds ahead, offshore or on.
Gentle wavelets look never to subside,
Performing relentlessly after dawn.

She's up and afire, growing higher,
Mariners now look to the sky.
Old tars and salts know the power,
The sun at dawn when night.

Donald Edward Webber

SUNSHINE

Sunshine doesn't come just in daytime,

Though many only find it that way.

Sometimes it comes in a warm smile,

For a most unexpected stay.

Receive it without really trying,

As happiness in one's eyes.

Feel it with open arms,

Before the moment flies.

Accept what you can, conditionless it's given.

Look well beyond your shroud.

For nature cushions the search for dreams,

Like rainbows in the clouds.

Donald Edward Webber

Little Lilly Littlefield

Innocence in Curiosity

Donald Edward Webber

Little Lilly Littlefield
Mountain Rose

Little Lilly Littlefield went looking for a flower,
She crossed a stream,
She climbed a hill,
Knowing of its power.

Little Lilly Littlefield, you see,
Was more perceptive than most.
"What might it make of me," she asked,
"If I became its host?"

Little Lilly Littlefield felt its velvet petal,
She smelled its sweet aroma, stroked its tender stem,
All when dreaming soundly,
Midst the urban din.

Little Lilly Littlefield, soon found the city's edge,
Now woods and trails,
And scents of pine,
Gave signs she would not fail.

For Little Lilly Littlefield,
Precocious some might say,
The flower contained a message,
Only a child could obey.

Donald Edward Webber

For Little Lilly Littlefield,
The search was just the first,
To answer many questions,
Of life and death and hurt.

Over a rise and abutting a stump,
Little Lilly envisioned her flower.
Grayish purple, the smell of lavender,
A Mountain Rose with herbal power.

Ran so fast, Lilly raced, to see the Mountain Rose,
Finally to embrace with care, her newly treasured find.
Then listened with intent, she did, her ear was to the bloom,
She heard the message saved for her, and surely all mankind.

For Little Lilly Littlefield, it was a new beginning.
The precious blossom breathed out loud,
Then spilled her pollen throughout.
Little Lilly's journey, it seems, was soon to be avowed.

Little Lilly Littlefield, smiled the biggest grin.
She felt the calm, she felt the wellness, Herbal Rose can bring.
"I'll tell the world, I'll sing its praises,
I'll make the bell towers ring."

Little Lilly Littlefield
My Soul

Little Lilly Littlefield went looking for her soul,

"It's in my mind or in my heart," so she had been told.

A bit confused as where to start, for some had called it spirit,

She stopped and breathed and started again, her feelings ever bold.

Little Lilly Littlefield, took to reading books,

Thought and self, desire and passion, were first where she would look.

One's essence too, came to light, when thinking of emotion,

But then she said "Do souls have mass? Must I think location?"

She thought of inner wisdom, a subject she didn't understand,

"Knowing" was another, a language she did not command.

"Is this a universe of souls, of consciousness as well?

I'll start with mind and intellect, while science tries to tell."

William James says souls exist, but calls it consciousness,

'States of insight into truths, full of significance.'

Illumination, revelation, inarticulate they remain,

Carrying a sense of authority, "Are soul and mind the same?"

Little Lilly Littlefield, more confused than before,

"What exists and what does not?" She studied themes of lore.

"And what about Ontology, is there a study of being?

Is that my soul, my mind, my purpose, all of this conceiving?"

Then she read Spinoza which helped direct her way,

Mind and body seemingly, are aspects of one name.

Both exist as attributes, of only one true kind,

God and nature, mind and body, certainly the same."

My soul, my spirit, my inner being,

Must rest within my heart.

You spoke to me my deepest self, I only need look there,

"I think, therefore I am," one said, "With that I now can share."

Little Lilly Littlefield
Nothingness

What is nothingness?
I truly don't understand.
Is it darkness, emptiness?
Can I hold it in my hand?

I can't imagine the void,
An endless hollow space.
Where does one find it?
Surely in a known place.

Some say we're sure to meet it,
Most certainly after we die.
How could we know we found it,
If that's where our future lies?

And how does anyone know,
If the answer rests in death?
No one has survived it,
At least, I think not yet.

Saint Augustine said death results,
From Adam's choice in Eden,
Original sin in the *Bible*, is that the ultimate cause?
If death equates to nothingness, it's time for me to pause.

If "Changelessness is death,"
Reads an old Chinese proverb,
Then nothingness can't be,
But an esoteric concept, which has no depth for me.

Buddha preached death, rebirth too,
Of the ego only, not the mortal body.
Still where is nothingness, no sin, no god, no soul?
Even Buddha's Nirvana is said to extinguish the whole.

Plato wrote of death, could it be nothingness,
Or a migration of the soul?
He even talked unconsciousness,
But defined it not for all.

Socrates wrote "Dreamless sleep,"
How comforting is that?
Who remembers anything,
With time and space aback?"

Robert Lanza wrote "Death is an illusion,"
I take it nothingness is too.
But that doesn't leave me an answer,
I truly do not have a clue.

Back to a definition,
"Non-existence" provides no support.
Epicurus wrote "Privation of all sentience,

No subjective experience, self-awareness, no brain function," he reports.

Giulio Tonni adds another view,
"Dissolve" into nothingness, for that is what we do.
"Plunge" into darkness, deems Thomas W. Clark,
"No awareness of space, no basis for time," end of life is due.

Where do I go to get an answer?
Nothingness is nothing for all I can tell.
Could it be I'll never know?
For that would be my hell.

Donald Edward Webber

LITTLE LILLY LITTLEFIELD
Thinking

"Think, do we?" Lilly asked,

"Any idea what that means?

Surely we do it,

But is thinking all that it seems?"

"We think, we reason," Little Lilly said,

"How fortunate is that?

But do we understand what we are doing,

Talking to one self feeling smart?"

"Rationale must come after reason," Lilly surmised,

"How else could we create?

That set us apart from lesser beings,

Superior we can pontificate."

"Words took shape after expression," Lilly figured out.

"Cro-Magnon named a tree a tree,

When once it was a shrug,

Meaningless to all before, all of course but she."

"Now a word, a picture in the mind,

Takes precedence over matter.

One sees, one knows, one feels, one hears,

When visuals overcome all banter."

"Suddenly awake, aware of one's surroundings,

All due to experience and perception.

You think, you feel, you have a sense about you,

Self-awareness, a product of evolution."

"Sensations, illuminations, revelations came,

Along with reflections to perceive."

Then thinking in terms of words, Lilly gathered,

"We developed complex ideas."

With a conscious mind, we became self-aware,

Born with a blank tablet, to a developed identity.

A question left asks Lilly, 'Where this is all stored?"

A question left asks Lilly, "Is this for all eternity?"

39

LITTLE LILLY LITTLEFIELD'S LITTLE BOOK OF POEMS

Donald Edward Webber

LITTLE LILLY LITTLEFIELD
"Who Am I?"

Little Lilly Littlefield asked about her life.

She approached each day with open eyes,

Amidst much trouble and strife.

Then ventured forth without reserve,

Bent not to slow when tired.

"Who am I," she said, "midst this conscious life?"

The question for the wise, "Just who am I,

A child of God, DNA, a simple carbon cell?

Or is it purely energy that brought me to this day?"

Einstein said he surely knew, and that was gravity.

Hawking claimed it was small waves, quantum being key.

"I'm lost in all of this," Lilly thought, "much too much formality."

We look to God, yet have lost trust, while science looks to energy,

Both are worn these centuries many, no facts with which to accompany.

"I think therefore I am," said Rene Descarte from France.

"Dare to understand yourself," the German Kant replied,

The universe began with purpose, so he surmised.

"Who are we and from where we come?" Lilly responds and sighs.

Little Lilly Littlefield found herself dismayed,

An answer key wasn't there, nothing was displayed.

Kierkegaard talked existential, a Dane with faith in God,

"Existence is encounter," from German Martin Buber.

Humanism, reformation, the answer from Martin Luther.

"And here I am, just a girl, more confused than others."

So many say "I know the way," including Lao-Tzu.

"Balance is the Tao," he said, 'the path to harmony."

Chopra wrote that time and space, of which we are apart,

Create along with nature, an enduring symphony."

"It's up to me since no one knows, just why we are alive.

I'll take along what thoughts I can, solely to survive."

What is de Chardin's Noosphere, the final human state?

Descarte's Cogito Ergo Sum, 'I think therefore I am',

Suggests more than human realm, suggests a final plan.

Muslims call for judgment, a final day of,

Christians call for heaven, looking up above.

Calvin writes there is no choice, man does not options,

We are predestined, he said, for hell or for salvation.

Donald Edward Webber

Hans Peter Durr talks quantum states,

Where we live after death.

John Hick writes of knowing God,

It's death that gives us rest.

Jeff Mason writes of death and portals,

Of which we speak so metaphorical.

Plato wrote of portals too, Socrates of four,

Moving into nothingness from this world or to more.

Little Lilly Littlefield ventured to the limit,

Answers yes, but never all, beyond the metaphysic.

"I think it's time to recognize, the limits of understanding,

Nothing guides me to resolve, an answer all commanding."

LITTLE LILLY LITTLEFIELD
"Why Am I Here?"

Little Lilly Littlefield went looking for a reason, "Why am I here?"

She wasn't depressed or unhappy, just curious when looking about.

Having dealt with the metaphysical question, "Who am I?"

She thought she might be enlightened, with a response she could

tout.

Little Lilly Littlefield, read Sermon on the Plain,

She took from it more than most, a posture to maintain.

Next she read *Leviticus*, Commandments 613?

"Whoa," she said, "I'll never see life as they explain."

Buddha talked of ego, for one must give it up,

Hindus detailed Karma, why life is in a caste.

Muslims spoke of submission, the meaning of the word,

Shinto practice rituals and adhere to them to last.

Lao-Tzu advocated piety, humility too,

Paul Tillich's goal, link man with God. "That's what we must do."

Apostle Paul wrote with passion, to heal and care for all,

Letters written in Biblical times, meant to prevent man's fall.

Donald Edward Webber

Little Lilly Littlefield, finally found her answer,

The works of Soren Kierkegaard, a Dane at night she read.

Life can only be, he said, understood when looking back,

Then he finalized the thought, it must be lived ahead.

Hooray for Lilly Littlefield, who's managing to find her way,

Due to many philosophers, even sages of the day.

Little Lilly Littlefield now knows what to do,

Live her life for others and serve humanity too.

Little Lilly Littlefield
X Marks the Spot

I've mused, I rambled,

I've carried on.

"Princess of Speculation,"

Maybe that's why I was born?

Answers to life, to death, and more,

Really can't be proven, so why go on?

Don't just agree as you read these words,

'Cause X marks the spot, the spot not yet seen.

X is a chromosome, surely you know,

So is Y but let's let that go.

What makes up an X might be an answer,

Smaller than an electron, my rejoinder.

Quantum mechanics - stay with me now,

And quantum gravity provide the clues,

To memory and consciousness, mind and soul,

Where they are kept, how they are used.

Fermions and bosons - what are they?

Donald Edward Webber

The smallest of particles, quantum physics say.

They are waves held together by gravity unmeasurable,

Waves held together by a force invariable.

Waves make up elements, one hundred and eighteen,

Yet waves are waves, not mass or matter.

Gluons bind waves, miniscule and moving,

Gravitons bind matter, larger and exacting.

Does biological activity produce our mind?

Does neural activity produce consciousness?

Science has answers not easy to find,

Mathematics looks to integration, an algorithm defined.

If fermions make quarks - three fermions I'm told,

Then quarks are waves with triple the power.

Triple the power makes hadrons and more,

Triple the capacity, maybe awareness is stored.

I'm Lilly Littlefield - probably lost you by now,

Too much espousing, too much to say.

But this I know after searching so long,

Consciousness and being, must rest in a quantum wave.

Donald Edward Webber

Dark Days

"The world breaks everyone and afterward many are strong at the broken places."

\-   Ernest Hemingway
A Farewell to Arms

Donald Edward Webber

BACK AGAIN

Back again,

Back to that hollow space called loneliness and fear.

Some call it heartbreak, some confusion,

Some call it, self-imposed illusion.

Traveling back to the same stark places,

To the shadows and strain of disconcerting faces.

Visiting one's compartments, how many there are,

Lost to reason for countless hours.

Being here too many times to count,

While avoiding without really trying.

Emptiness brings a soul almost crying,

A hopelessness too deep to surmount.

Back again,

One senses it's not the last.

No longer escaping or forgetting pain,

Hopelessly trapped in the past.

Donald Edward Webber

CAN YOU SEE IN THE MORN?

Can you see in the morn,

Where you are going through the day?

Do you expect roadblocks,

And where they might lay?

Does sunrise surprise you,

When expecting clouds?

What bright light blinds you,

While peering through shrouds?

So daylight exposes you,

For the fool you have been?

What else serve as reminders,

Of all you did when?

What of dark, the color of night,

How hollow is your fear and fright?

Moonless skies beckon when stark,

Wasting ones strength, reserve, and might.

Donald Edward Webber

And why doesn't evening, end of exposure,

To the soul, bring shelter and relief?

Quiet ensues, when neon stops flashing,

Is there still, no respite from grief?

HOW LONG?

How long does pain last,

Is there a conclusion?

Days, weeks, months, years,

All seem like an illusion.

Wouldn't have begun seeking answers,

If not for so many that cared.

Still dragging too many chains tho,

Heart and soul stay bared.

Does reality override depression,

Does truth drag one down?

Most answers avoid conclusion,

Alone that is profound.

Question progress, acceptable change,

A forward move then stumble back.

Process is long, however arranged,

Pain stays in place, remains a fact.

Donald Edward Webber

I CAN NOT SEND FLOWERS

I cannot send flowers,
Not even a card,
How I'd like to take you to dinner and a show.

Just know that I know,
Just know that I care,
You are my love forever, deservedly so.

How we arrived here,
How it came to be,
Remains a mystery, deep inside of me.

Memories are left,
Thoughts sustained,
Of days with you, with passion they came.

When first found,
Two making a life,
Foreign were words like sickness and strife.

Reality soon, it set in,
With a grip too tight for any to win,
But soon new adventures hopefully begin.

I cannot send flowers,
Not even a card,
Surely again someday, no matter the pain.

LONELINESS DOES NOT HAVE A CHAMPION

Maybe it's the dark days, damp and dreary,
When loneliness truly sets in?
A chill in the air, feelings of despair,
Sensing where one might have been.

Could it be night, solitude and silence,
When weariness settles in?
Sounds from afar, at the window the stars,
Reminders of loss of friends.

Would it be Sundays, afternoons alone,
When emptiness makes it way in?
Couples at play, families in tow,
Leaving you alone midst the din.

Should it be never, sometimes it's always,
When hopelessness works its way in?
Feelings of remiss, so hard to dismiss,
Loneliness does not have a champion.

Donald Edward Webber

THE WORLD IS CHANGING

The world is changing, changing now.
Not certain why, not certain how.
Just know in the mirror, the man you see,
Is not the same, he used to be.

Where is the confidence, once one could feel?
Missing is the strength, that truly was real.
Where is the character that carried a name?
Missing is integrity, he proudly claimed.

Friends were lost with whom he could share,
Family he had that accepted his care.
Business was pleasure eagerly sought,
Holidays many, how comfortably brought.

Seems no longer hiding the loss,
Demeanor and style reflect the cost.
Struggle to fit, to share, to care,
Not the same, when one's soul is bare.

A life need rebuilding, a change is due,
With that one can't argue, believe it is true.
No longer fooling all he knows,
Naïve it would be to think it so.

Donald Edward Webber

THINK YOU KNOW?

Think you know, how quickly they come,

Feelings so void and empty?

Like a sudden lift in the road,

Light head, stomach heavy.

Think you know, how drained one feels,

Tired and spent of energy?

If only to drop where one stands,

Eyes closed, with thoughts empty.

Meaningless it seems, "Acts being seven ages."

Where does that leave you, when closer to the end?

Scars and pain, disappointing intimacies,

Lost loves, broken hearts, entropy.

Work and toil and for what, they ask?

Forget a name, avoid an acquaintance,

Too many friends not recognized.

Job, Job, if only for your patience?

Moses, my friend, took into his hands,

Donald Edward Webber

The search for promise, new beginnings,

Climbed a mountain, set the rules,

Even asked for life's ending.

Ebenezer may have had it right,

His words echo yet.

"If they would rather die," he said,

"They had better do it."

The Kids in Us and Then Some
"Hey kids, what time is it? It's Howdy Doody time!"

"Buffalo" Bob Smith
1947 – 1960

Artwork: Lindsay Kesslen

Donald Edward Webber

AN OLD CABIN IN THE RAIN

Calming patter on the roof,
Steady, in harmony with my thoughts.
Only rafters and beams separate us,
Rain from my head on a pillow.

An open book on my chest,
Feeling heat from the light on the bed stand.
Dampness wanting to invade my comfort,
But for warmth from birch on the iron grate below.

No ceiling, only the ridge board atop,
Allowing assuring sounds of safety.
Magical, the splashing on windows,
Gentle, the beats remaining above.

Lying in the loft, able to touch splintered logs,
Hypnotic, the continuous splatter above.
Up steady comes the energy of the burn,
Wintergreen and leathery, smells of the fire.

Escaping to the old book, smells musty,
Eyes closed before each turned page.
The calm, the restfulness, peace,
An old cabin in the rain.

Published in *Frost Meadow Review, Volume 4*

Donald Edward Webber

FLY FISHING

Braced in swift water up to the knees,

While steady underfoot to cast,

A motion so fluid, certain, true,

Practiced over seasons to last.

Shoulders move deftly with purpose,

A power few can afford,

Wrists don't bend or wander,

Arm serves to guide back and forth.

Line retrieves directly,

Straightening behind the back,

Rolling to the stream in an instant,

Delivering a fly to a hatch.

Ten to one, ten to one,

Movement like a clock.

Casting back, casting back,

Nearing a swirl by a rock.

Soon on the water there's commotion,

A Rainbow is in the air.

Line is taut, pole is bent,

The trout is played with care.

Only minutes to land,

Much less to dispatch.

Then taking but seconds, brace and stand,

Cast back, cast back, to the hatch.

Edited by Rich Burnham, Wolfeboro, New Hampshire

Donald Edward Webber

HEADING UPSTREAM TO SPAWN

Watch the illusive salmon,

When heading upstream to spawn,

They dart, they slue, hide midst rocks,

When my shadow blocks the sun.

Hiking upstream with leaves underfoot,

Delivers hundreds of crackles and pops.

Colors of fall shimmer in the sun,

Light on the water seems to hop.

Salmon Salar Sebago,

Your silver metallic sheen,

Sure to bring one singing reels,

Flipping and leaping in dreams.

Salmon of course are wily,

And be certain, hard to catch.

But 'tis the season of spawning,

They're safe 'til hatchlings hatch.

How many times can you clean your beds,

Two or four or more?

The spawn is repetition,

Akin to my inner core.

A unique sensory fingerprint,

Passed on in genes to fry,

Calls to return to home waters,

Some adults swim up to die.

Soon to complete the journey,

Gliding downstream with ease,

Salmon's encounter with nature,

Falls mission before the freeze.

Edited by Rich Burnham, Wolfeboro, New Hampshire

Donald Edward Webber

I HATE TO FLY

And why shouldn't I?

Seats are narrow, leg room is poor,

One's herded through the gate area, delayed at the door.

Food is awful if at all, circulated air is much too dry,

Clothes are wrinkled, one's day is awry.

One flight is canceled, another is late,

Schedules are not certain to any State.

Terminals are no better than bus stations of old,

Cabins can be hot or unreasonably cold.

Commuter flights are even worse,

Can't stand up, trip on a purse.

Carry an umbrella in case it rains,

Otherwise one's wet and clothes are stained.

The back seat is the worse seat, it doesn't recline,

Yet pilots and attendants don't seem to mind.

No place for my coat, and often my bag,

Now one's subject to the little red tag.

Noise from the props, only hurts the ears,

And humps on the floor put stress on the knees.

Tired of pretzels, peanuts, and mix,

Tired of inconvenience airlines won't fix.

Attendants are tired, pilots force a big Hi!

Please provide me an alternative to the friendly sky.

Donald Edward Webber

LOOKING FOR HIM

Looking for him well into the night,

Looking for him at ten, eleven, even midnight.

Know what he looks like, pictures are everywhere,

Know what he looks like, jolly, fat, red faced where bare.

Listening a while to the roof and the eaves,

Listening a while to wind, sky, even trees.

Thought he might be fooled, wouldn't expect my waiting,

Thought he might be fooled, carrying so much through the grating.

Waiting and watching, with an eye on the tree,

Waiting and watching, closed eyes felt good to me.

Noise made me jump, looking all around,

Noise made me jump, bows, boxes, toys abound.

Not disappointed, after all he was here.

Not disappointed, stay awake longer, no nap next year.

73

LITTLE LILLY LITTLEFIELD'S LITTLE BOOK OF POEMS

Donald Edward Webber

OLD DOGS FALL IN LOVE TOO

Old dogs admire beauty, found in every flower,
Blooms, petals, pollen puffed in the air.
Maybe boys wouldn't take time to do so,
When young and forging ahead.
Maybe they couldn't do so later,
When building a homestead.

Old dogs love perfumes, designed to allure,
Fragrant, mellow, enticing as they should.
Young men did earlier,
When most eager in youth,
They did much earlier,
When sharing with another they could.

Old dogs treasure velvet, silk, cashmere,
Gentle, fragile, draped softly and loose.
Seems old dogs always have,
But didn't take note,
To an old dog they were givens,
"Should-have-beens," to expect.

Old dogs like symphonies, opera, big bands,
Complexity, arrangement, depth and demands.
Youth never paid attention,
Boys listened from afar,
Youth never gave mention,
Too unappreciative, young men are.

Old dogs take to whiskey, cigars, even gin,
What once was not acceptable, no longer is sin.
Maybe a carryover from younger times,
Thoughts of a calming, tranquil day.
Surely a carryover from innocent times,
Resting and sleeping, holding demons at bay.

Old dogs fall in love, surely you know,
Certainly not surprising how.
Old passions, desires might not be the drive,
Though hormones and senses remain yet alive.
It could be a smile, a cheek-to-cheek kiss,
Reminding old dogs of just what they miss.

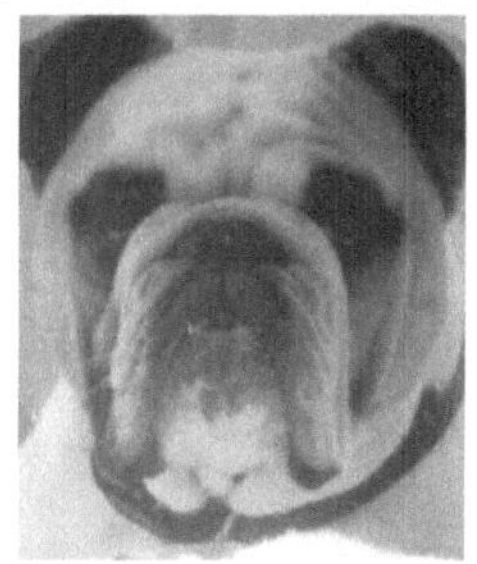

Donald Edward Webber

SOUND OF A TRAIN AT NIGHT

Listen to the sound of train at night,
When far away and out of sight,
Her whistle blows hollow, lonely, afar,
A whistle in the night, under the stars.

Echoes from rails, the bells, the gates,
Clickety-click, and clack-clack-clack.
Shrills from the steel, bells at the gates,
Coupling, screeching of metal brakes,

Rumbles in the house, sounds like thunder,
Waiting for the caboose, coupled in back.
Stirring excitement, adventure, and fright,
Sounds of a train passing through night.

Did you hear it before many years ago,
When just in youth, what did you know?
Where is your stick, your red hanky sack,
Your sandwich and apple, what more need you pack?

When all is gone, silence envelopes sight,
Know that dreams only blur the light.
Sounds will come time and again,
Count the nights, many more times when.

Donald Edward Webber

SOUNDS OF SUMMER

In bed, breathing rhythmically,
Just listening, the window ajar,
The sounds of summer,
Close and afar.

A wisp of cool air
Coming from, I don't know where,
Rustles the curtains, refreshes the room,
Stirring fading senses, asleep but aware.

Highway's a distance, a droning din,
Hot tires on the freeway sing in the night,
Big engine cars rev heavy out of the light,
Capturing the essence of sound over sight.

Couples return unaware of their voices,
Carrying through window, neighborhood and street.
Laughter and romance, alive in their choices,
Hand in hand meandering, each step carries a beat.

Kids out late, wonderful their laughter,
Sticks used as canes, maybe as swords.
Innocence is beautiful, away from home,
Especially when playing knights and lords.

Kids built a tent in the backyard once more,
Brothers and sisters with flashlights explore.
How fun the sound of darkness so near,
How fun the sound, when nothing to fear?

Lights in the driveway, a U-turn and gone,
A train on the tracks, most evenings then dawn.
A siren reminds, all the streets are alive,
Full moon or not, full-days move on.

The cat's on the sill, my retriever is aware,
At night I query, why would they care?
Back on the bed, you curious two,
Come the morning, plenty to do.

Donald Edward Webber

THEY WOKE ON A SUNDAY

They woke on a Sunday with thoughts of play,
Until they heard Mother's "Church today!"
IPods and cell phones would have to wait,
Until they returned even if late.

Soon they were rushing to dress and prepare,
While parents seemed anxious with burdens to bear.
Breakfast was a Sunday's and clothes were too,
Then off to church and its own school.

Into a service they didn't understand,
They felt their Mother's comforting hand.
Shortly thereafter they ran to their class,
With teachers and friends and pencils at last.

Something about managers brightened by stars,
Would stay with them past the next few hours.
Something of Magi out of the East,
Would stay with them long into next week.

They ate Sunday dinner with thoughts away,
Until they heard Mother "Time to play!"
Legos and texts didn't have to wait,

Better get going before it's too late.

But thoughts of mangers covered with straw,
Seemed to stay with with them no matter how far.
They thought past church's long first hour,
There's more to the story than just a bright star.

Donald Edward Webber